ZBrush Tutorial Guide

The Definitive User Manual To Master
ZBrush with Illustrations

By

Isaac Alejo

Table of Contents

INTRODUCTION

Z Brush emerged as a distinctive tool, allowing users to create illustrations in a unique two-and-a-half-dimensional style.

Over the past year, there has been a significant transformation in the ZBrush user community. This change has been particularly evident in my Introduction to Digital Sculpting class at the Gnomon School of Visual Effects in Hollywood. Students are now drawn to ZBrush not only for character design in movies, broadcasting, and video games, but also for a range of other creative purposes. This expanding community includes jewelry designers, toy sculptors, visual effects and environment creators, matte painters, illustrators, and fine art artists. The intention behind this book was to make ZBrush accessible to a diverse group of practitioners across various fields.

The purpose of this book is to help you become proficient with the software and use it confidently. After reading this book, I hope you'll be motivated to explore more advanced resources.

CHAPTER 1: DIGITAL ART BASICS

An Introduction to ZBrush

Entering a fully stocked artist's studio, you'll discover cabinets and drawers brimming with an assortment of paints and brushes, a large canvas, a closet filled with every imaginable sculpting medium, a lighting setup, camera, light box, projector, kiln, maquette armatures, and an extensive collection of carving and cutting tools—all meticulously organized for optimal workflow. This is ZBrush, an all-inclusive studio enabling digital creation of paintings, sculptures, and their combinations. What's more, ZBrush's versatility extends beyond its own confines, allowing easy import of 3D models and 2D textures from other applications. Serving as a standalone digital art workspace or an integral part of production pipelines for video games, films, and toy manufacturing, ZBrush's utilization has evolved over time.

Initially, ZBrush was primarily employed for crafting and modifying digital models that were subsequently animated and rendered in other 3D software like Autodesk® Maya®, 3ds Max®, Cinema 4D, and modo. While this remains true, ZBrush's influence has spread to various industries. In the realm of film, artists favor ZBrush due to its unique capability to handle dense models with millions of polygons. This permits the creation of intricate organic details, such as wrinkles, pores, scars, and more, that conventional 3D software struggles to replicate. These details can be incorporated directly into the model or exported as bump and displacement textures for use in other rendering software, leading to incredibly realistic virtual objects. Notable studios like ILM, Gentle Giant, Weta, and Sony Pictures Imageworks have harnessed ZBrush's potential to craft characters and scenes in blockbuster films.

Recently, ZBrush's applications have expanded to fields beyond animation and effects. It has found utility in crafting toys, game characters and environments, medical visualization, jewelry design, concept design, and even physical sculpture creation. Artists employ ZBrush to design models on computers, then transform them into tangible forms through 3D printing technology, foreseeing its integration into desktop fabrication pipelines as 3D printing becomes more accessible.

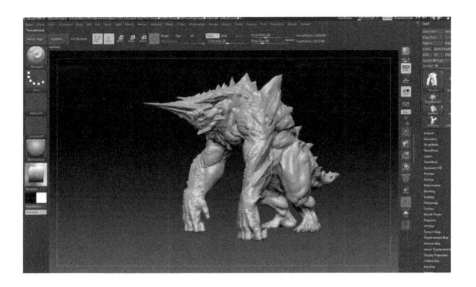

ZBrush's versatility extends to digital illustrations as well, offering sculpting, painting, and rendering tools, along with unique rendering technology. Within ZBrush, artists can create custom virtual materials that simulate realistic surfaces or artistic styles, responding to virtual lights and shadows when rendered. The program's compatibility with 2D paint software like Adobe Photoshop and Corel Painter further enhances its capabilities. Seamless exchange of digital 3D models and 2D images between these programs empowers artists to push creative boundaries, firmly establishing ZBrush as an essential component of the digital artist's toolkit.

Understanding digital images

Anatomy of a pixel

A pixel is a colored square on the screen with specific position information. When combined, pixels create a raster graphic. Each pixel contains color and position data stored in memory. If you enlarge or zoom in on a raster graphic, you can see the individual pixels that make up the image.

The digital image file stores pixel positions using x- and y-coordinates, representing horizontal and vertical positions, respectively. When you zoom or scroll in the software, the pixel positions change relative to the screen, but the software keeps track of their positions relative to the entire image.

The word "jagged" appears jagged due to visible square pixels along the curved edges, called aliasing. Conversely, the word "smooth" appears smooth because of an anti-aliasing technique that blends pixels of varying lightness along the curved edges.

Channels and Color Depth

In addition to positional data, pixels contain information on how to display colors. Computer screens use red, green, and blue light to create colors. A pixel with 100 percent red, 0 percent blue, and 0 percent green appears red, while a pixel with 50 percent red, 50 percent blue, and 0 percent green looks purple. All three values at 0 percent create a black pixel, and at 100 percent, the pixel appears white.

Color depth refers to the amount of color information stored for each pixel in an image. Grayscale images only retain black, white, and shades of gray, typically 256 levels. This results in a black-and-white image with reduced data storage.

While traditional painting considers red, yellow, and blue as primary colors, computer screens treat red, green, and blue as the primary ones. Mixing red and green produces the secondary color yellow. An RGB image stores red, green, and blue information in separate channels, each containing the values (or percentages) for their respective colors in every pixel. For a demonstration, you can explore RGB values using ZBrush's color chooser.

To embark on a colorful journey with ZBrush, follow these steps:

1. Launch ZBrush.

   Access the Color palette by clicking on "Color" in the menu bar.

2. Navigate the color selector area by dragging your cursor.

3. Observe the dynamic R, G, and B numeric values below the color area. These values adjust based on the blend required to achieve the selected color. Note that each channel's highest value is 255, and the lowest is 0.

4. Fine-tune the color by clicking and selecting the R, G, and B sliders, then inputting specific numeric values. For instance, setting R to 255, G to 0, and B to 255 results in a radiant fuchsia hue.

Moving into the realm of RGBA format, an intriguing fourth channel, the alpha channel, emerges. This channel stores information on pixel opacity, granting images regions of transparency.

Color depth refers to the level of information employed in each color channel. Computers rely on bits, binary entities of 1s and 0s, to store data. A 24-bit RGB image assigns 8 bits to each channel (3 × 8 = 24). This enables each 8-bit channel to hold 256 shades of color, resulting in a staggering 16 million colors for the entire image. For a 32-bit RGBA image, an additional 8 bits are dedicated to the alpha channel.

As the number of bits increases, so does the image's capacity for storing information and displaying a broader range of colors. However, higher-bit images demand more memory for storage and processing. Interestingly, an image with 16 bits per channel (48 bits for RGB, 64 bits for RGBA) may be confusingly referred to as a 16-bit image, in contrast to a 16-bit (5 bits per channel) high-color image. The world of computer terminology can be bewildering, but with experience, you'll grow accustomed to these intricacies. Despite computers' logical nature, the humans who create and utilize them sometimes navigate a labyrinth of understanding. If you're an artist in television or film production, you'll find yourself working with 16-bit (per channel) images more frequently than 16-bit (5 bits per channel) high-color images.

Image Formats

Digital images can be stored in various formats, each representing a specific arrangement of information within a file. Common image formats include TIFF, JPEG, and GIF.

Many software programs have their own native document formats. For instance, Photoshop uses PSD format, Corel's Painter uses RIFF format, and ZBrush has its unique ZBR document format.

Image formats can be compressed to save storage space. Certain formats like JPEG and GIF come with built-in compression, while others like SGI offer the option for compression or no compression. However, compression can lead to a loss in image quality, resulting in blurry, grainy, or inaccurate colors, especially noticeable in images viewed on the internet.

Compression can be categorized as lossy, causing diminished image quality, or lossless, which reduces file size without significant quality loss. Lossless formats like PNG tend to produce larger files compared to lossy formats. Video sequences also utilize compression.

Understanding file formats and compression becomes vital when working with computer graphics, be it images in ZBrush or textures and alphas for 3D models in other applications. Compressed images used as texture sources or sculpting tools can lead to lower model quality. Additionally, various 3D applications and rendering engines may prefer specific formats, which is crucial knowledge when exporting images from ZBrush for use in other software. Deeper insights into image manipulation in ZBrush will be covered later in this book.

Vector Images

Computers can utilize vectors to generate digital images. Vector graphics are created through mathematical formulas and calculations performed by the computer and its software. The output of these computations yields smooth lines and shapes, often filled with colors. One of the key advantages of vector graphics is their ability to be continuously drawn and updated when the image is scaled, moved, or rotated, ensuring consistent quality regardless of size or position.

Popular vector graphic programs like Adobe Illustrator and Adobe Flash are widely used. Vectors are also employed in modeling interfaces to represent 3D objects in packages such as Maya and 3ds Max, with special rendering engines capable of producing vector graphics as final outputs. However, ZBrush does not support direct creation of vector images, and this discussion on vectors concludes here.

Understanding resolution is of utmost importance when working with ZBrush. Yet, computer resolution can be a perplexing concept due to the various terminologies and measurement methods involved. Throughout this book, we will revisit this topic frequently, so there's no need to worry if you haven't fully mastered the concept by the end of this section.

Resolution essentially denotes the density of information within a specific area. In computer graphics, it is often associated with the number of pixels packed into a portion of the screen. However, resolution can also pertain to the number of polygons or points within a segment of a 3D model. The resolution of your computer screen affects how your images are displayed and created. When applying a 2D image texture to a 3D model, considering both the pixel resolution of the 2D image and the polygon resolution of the 3D model is crucial to achieve satisfactory results. In ZBrush, you will frequently engage in such tasks, so keeping resolution in mind is essential.

Understanding resolution

Screen resolution

Screen resolution refers to the number of square-sized pixels appearing on the screen, measured both horizontally and vertically. The physical screen size is often described diagonally, like a 22-inch monitor, measuring from one corner to the opposite corner.

Your screen can display text and images in various resolutions, set through the operating system's control panel or system preferences. Screen resolution is represented as the number of pixels available horizontally multiplied by the number available vertically. Common resolutions include 640x480, an older standard for smaller monitors; 720x486, the United States broadcast television standard; and 1920x1080, used for high-definition television (HDTV).

Screen resolution impacts how ZBrush appears on your screen. Lower resolutions provide less space for the ZBrush interface and documents, prompting many graphics artists to invest in larger monitors or use multiple monitors.

Document resolution

Moving on to document resolution, when you zoom in on a digital image in a graphics program, you can observe individual pixels composing the image. However, the actual screen pixels don't change in size, and you don't alter your computer's hardware resolution. Instead, the graphics program enables you to view a higher magnification of the image, exceeding the document's native resolution.

For instance, a 320x240 document set at 200 percent magnification is displayed at 640x480, utilizing four times as many monitor pixels for each document pixel, resulting in a blocky appearance. Conversely, when you zoom out, the number of displayed pixels is halved. Zooming is a useful feature for working on image details, but it creates a disparity between document and screen resolutions. Hence, when working with computer images, it's crucial to consider the document resolution, regardless of how it appears on the screen.

Document resolution is typically described in dots per inch (dpi), sometimes called pixels per inch (ppi), even in metric system countries. An image displayed on a computer monitor at 100 percent resolution is usually 72 dpi. However, images intended for print require higher resolutions, usually at least 300 dpi, and often between 600 and 1200 dpi for commercial printing.

Image resolution

When conversing with 3D texture artists, you'll frequently encounter terms like "2K texture map." This phrase refers to an image with dimensions of 2048 pixels × 2048 pixels. To most people, "2K" would mean two thousand, but in the realm of computer graphics artists, "2K" translates to 2048. This is because texture images often have resolutions that are powers of 2. Consequently, 1K equals 1024 (210), 4K equals 4096 (212), and 512 (29) signifies an image size of 512 × 512.

In the context of texture artists, these images are always square. However, if you step into a production facility and they ask you to render an animation at 2K, providing them with a square 2048 × 2048 image sequence might not be well-received. This is because, in production terms, "2K" actually means 2048 pixels × 1556 pixels, which isn't truly 2K (nor square). In this context, "2K" stands for "2K Academy," a standardized film resolution.

The terminology may not seem entirely logical or consistent, but it all hinges on context. For the scope of this book, focusing on ZBrush, we'll use the language of texture artists, where "2K" means 2048 × 2048. However, if you venture into animation software like Maya, be aware that "2K" may carry different meanings depending on the context. To ensure clarity, it's best to ask for specific details from the people you're communicating with. Jargon may be beloved by geeks, but more often than not, it can hinder rather than aid understanding.

Polygon Resolution

Resolution can also refer to the number of points or polygons that constitute a 3D model. While I'll delve into polygons in greater detail later in this chapter, it's essential to grasp that the surface of a 3D model is formed by geometric shapes defined by three or more points (ZBrush restricts polygons to three or four points, but other modeling programs allow polygons with more points). By subdividing the polygons of a model, its smoothness is enhanced, enabling intricate details to be sculpted onto the surface.

In ZBrush, a model can consist of an immense number of polygons. Due to ZBrush's unique memory handling, these high-resolution models can be edited with significantly less performance slowdown compared to other 3D applications. Additionally, ZBrush stores multiple levels of subdivision resolution within a single model file, permitting you to adjust the 3D geometry's resolution while you work and export the same model at various resolutions for use in other 3D animation software.

Understanding 3D space

Anatomy of a Polygon

In computer graphics, there's no actual 3D object. Instead, we work with two-dimensional representations of three-dimensional objects on a computer screen. When we refer to 3D, it means a virtual object existing on a 2D screen with additional depth information along the z-axis. These virtual objects are made of polygons, which can be manipulated and animated. Other types of 3D geometry, like NURBS and subdivision surfaces, are converted to polygons during rendering. The number of polygons affects the object's smoothness and level of detail. ZBrush, for example, can handle millions of polygons, enabling artists to sculpt detailed digital clay smoothly. Normals play a vital role in working with polygon geometry, and they can be stored in a special texture called a normal map to add detail to lower-density models during rendering.

CHAPTER 2: UNDERSTANDING THE ZBRUSH INTERFACE

The Zen of ZBrush

If you haven't dabbled in 3D modeling or animation before, you might approach ZBrush with a slight advantage over those familiar with programs like Autodesk® Maya®, Autodesk® 3ds Max®, or XSI. ZBrush offers unique tools different from typical 3D modeling and animation software, potentially making it more accessible for beginners. Experienced 3D modelers might feel uneasy initially, as ZBrush doesn't follow the conventional 3D space environment. To get the best experience with ZBrush, it's essential to let go of preconceived notions about how a 3D program works. Instead, view ZBrush as a digital sculpting and painting workshop rather than a typical 3D modeling, painting, or texturing program.

The ZBrush Canvas

The canvas, which dominates the program's center. This square space is where you create your digital art, whether it's a digital painting, a three-dimensional sculpture, or a combination of both. The canvas in ZBrush is unique due to its height, width (y- and x-axes), and depth (z-axis) properties, giving rise to the name "ZBrush." When using a tool to paint a brush stroke on the canvas, you can manipulate its position in space, placing it in front of or behind other brush strokes. The default gradient on the canvas indicates the depth dimension.

The canvas serves as a platform for creating digital illustrations through brush strokes or as a virtual sculpting stand for molding digital clay into any imaginable shape. Furthermore, the canvas enables integrating sculptures into illustrations.

An illustration crafted on the canvas is known as a ZBrush document, which can be saved in the ZBR format or exported to various formats, including Adobe Photoshop. On the other hand, a digital sculpture created on the canvas is referred to as a mesh or a 3D tool, which can be saved in the ZTL format or exported in 3D model formats such as OBJ or Maya ASCII (.ma). To manage multiple elements, ZBrush allows saving them in a single file called a ZProject, using the ZPR file format. ZProjects function similarly to scenes in other 3D animation software, preserving the current state of tools, lighting, materials, and other elements for easy retrieval when reloading the project. Throughout our tour, I'll highlight how to save documents, 3D tools, and ZProjects.

Light Box

This appears at the top of the ZBrush canvas when you launch the program. To toggle Light Box visibility, press the comma (",") key on your keyboard. Its name draws inspiration from the light tables photographers use to examine their photographic negatives.

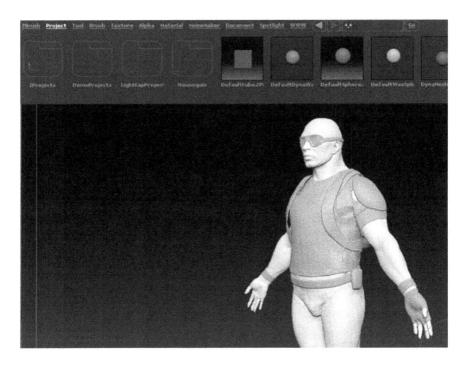

The purpose of Light Box is to provide easy access to files within the Pixologic directory structure on your computer's hard drive. This eliminates the need to navigate through your operating system's browsers, making it convenient to load the files you require for your ZBrush creations. Light Box offers sample files shipped with ZBrush as well as your own creations.

The menu at the top of Light Box serves as a link to directories within the Pixologic folder on your hard drive, encompassing ZBrushes, ZTools, ZAlphas, ZMaterials, ZTextures, and ZProjects folders. By clicking the Project link, you can view icons representing files within the ZProjects folder. Saving your files in this folder allows them to appear under the Project heading in Light Box. Similarly, saving files in the ZTools folder places them under the Tool heading.

To load a file, double-click (or quickly double-tap with a stylus on your digital tablet) an icon.

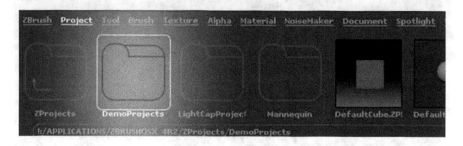

For instance, you can load the DemoSoldier.ZPR project by following the steps outlined. Projects in ZBrush are self-contained scenes, so loading one will close any currently open files, triggering a warning.

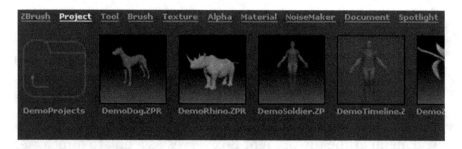

However, loading other types of files such as tools, materials, or brushes from Light Box will simply add them to your current ZBrush session.

You can perform searches within the displayed folder in Light Box by typing a search term in the field at the top, next to the menu bar. Adding an asterisk, like typing "Default∗," tells ZBrush to search for all files in the Project folder starting with "Default." To initiate the search, click the Go button or press the Enter/Return key. As you progress through this book, you'll have ample practice using Light Box, so don't worry if some details aren't entirely clear yet.

The ZBrush Shelves

To adjust the height of the Light Box display, you can click one of the four stack icons located at the far right of the Light Box menu. When you change the height, the icons within Light Box automatically rearrange themselves to fit the new setting, which is beneficial when dealing with numerous files in the folder.

Furthermore, the New button at the far right allows you to stack an additional Light Box strip on top of the current one. This enables you to have multiple Light Box strips open, each displaying the contents of a different folder. You can try clicking the New button and switch to the Tool folder, and then add a third strip displaying the contents of the Brush folder.

If you wish to remove a strip, simply click the Close button.

Above and on either side of the canvas, you'll find shelves holding the ZBrush buttons and controls.

We'll explore these shelves by moving from left to right around the canvas.

The Shelf on the Left

The left shelf in ZBrush contains buttons that open fly-out libraries of frequently accessed items during a typical editing session. These fly-out libraries, from top to bottom, include sculpting brushes, stroke types, alphas, textures, material shaders, color picker, and color swatches (color 1 and color 2).

The sculpting brushes are used for editing 3D meshes, but to utilize them, the mesh must be in Edit mode; otherwise, the sculpting brush icon is grayed out, and the fly-out library is inaccessible. You can view the contents of the sculpting brush library by following the steps provided in the instructions.

The fly-out library contains numerous preset sculpting brushes that come with ZBrush, allowing you to shape, pose, and detail your meshes. Throughout the book, you'll learn how to use these brush presets and even create and save custom ones.

By holding the mouse pointer over an icon, you can see an enlarged view of the brush and its name, which is a variation of a few base brush types. You can reduce the list of brushes in the fly-out library by typing the first letter of a brush name while the fly-out is open, making it easier to switch between brushes.

Moving down the left shelf, underneath the brush library, you'll find the stroke type fly-out library. The stroke type modifies the behavior of the current brush, and you can change it for the current brush by choosing one of the stroke type icons available in the library.

Below the stroke type fly-out is the alpha fly-out library, which contains grayscale images used for various purposes, often adding effects to sculpting brushes. Alphas function similarly to different nozzles added to cake decorating tools, altering the shape of frosting as applied to a cake.

Next is the textures fly-out library, where you can apply color images to sculpting brushes and 3D models, offering numerous creative possibilities. Like alphas, textures can be imported, exported, and used for different purposes.

Following that is the material presets fly-out library, allowing you to select materials that determine the surface quality of objects on the canvas. Each material affects factors like shininess, roughness, reaction to light effects, and even adds color to objects.

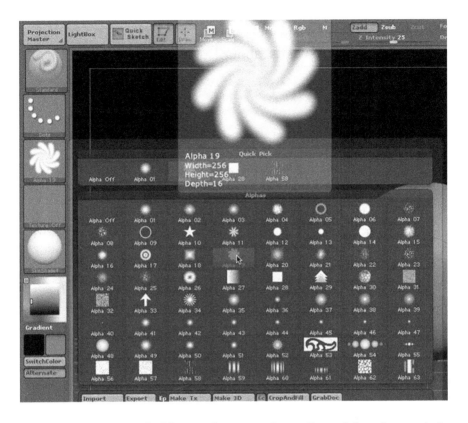

Below the materials library button, the color picker is a mini-interface for choosing different colors with RGB values, and it has two swatches for holding the main and secondary colors in memory.

The Shelf at the Top

Above the canvas, on the top shelf, there are several buttons arranged from left to right in four sections. The first section comprises buttons labeled Projection Master, Light Box, and Quick Sketch. However, the Quick Sketch and Projection

Master plug-ins may not be fully understood until you've acquired more knowledge about ZBrush.

The Light Box button allows you to toggle the visibility of Light Box. On the other hand, the Edit mode button activates sculpting brushes to modify a mesh on the canvas. When Edit mode is off, ZBrush enters Paint mode, where drawing on the canvas merely places copies of your meshes. While this is useful for creating illustrations, it can be confusing when attempting to sculpt a model.

Next to the Edit button, you'll find the Draw, Move, Scale, and Rotate buttons. When the Draw button is active, the current brush either draws a stroke on the canvas or, while editing a 3D model, lets you use the sculpting brushes to shape the model.

The behavior of the Move, Scale, and Rotate buttons varies depending on whether you're working on a 3D mesh in Edit mode or adding strokes to an illustration. Throughout the book, we'll extensively use these buttons, allowing you to understand their different functions clearly. At this moment, consider them as tools to position objects drawn on the canvas. The hotkeys for these functions are W for Move, E for Scale, and R for Rotate.

Moving on to the third section of the top shelf, there is a series of buttons and sliders. If these buttons are grayed out, ensure that the Draw button on the top shelf is activated. The buttons are labeled Mrgb, Rgb, and M. "M" stands for material, and "Rgb" represents the red, green, blue color channels. Essentially, these buttons select different painting modes: Mrgb allows painting material and color, Rgb allows painting only color, and M allows painting only material. Below these buttons, there is a slider that controls the intensity of the color contributed by the current brush. If none of these buttons are activated, the brush's effect on the canvas will be determined by the settings applied by the next set of buttons.

A similar triad of buttons follows, labeled Zadd, Zsub, and Zcut. They determine whether a sculpting brush raises the surface of a 3D tool (Zadd) or pushes it down (Zsub). ZCut is used solely for strokes or models that have been "dropped" onto the canvas, meaning they have been converted to a 2.5D illustration after switching out of Edit mode. The Z intensity slider controls how much the brush's strokes raise, lower, or cut into the surface of the 3D tool. If none of these buttons are activated, the brush may simply be set to paint color, material, or both without altering the 3D tool. These settings also influence the behavior of paint strokes when creating an illustration on the canvas.

At the top, the Best Preview Render (BPR) mode can be activated in ZBrush, offering higher-quality rendering compared to the default Preview mode. BPR includes shadows, improved anti-aliasing, and various effects like ambient occlusion, transparency, and subsurface scattering. Keep in mind that BPR rendering takes more time than the default Preview mode. ZBrush also provides other render options like Flat, Fast, Preview, and Best.

The SPix slider located below the BPR button controls the anti-aliasing quality for the render in Best Preview Render mode.

To navigate the canvas, you can use the Scroll and Zoom controls. Zooming in may cause jagged edges in the strokes on the canvas, similar to zooming into an image in Photoshop.

There are two buttons, Actual and AAHalf, that allow you to snap the canvas to 100 percent and 50 percent size, respectively. This helps improve the model's appearance and smoothens the anti-aliasing along the edges when rendering.

On the right shelf, there are three buttons to control object display on the canvas. The Persp button enables perspective distortion, while 3D meshes are typically displayed in isometric view. Using the perspective button can enhance the mesh's appearance, making it look more natural.

The Floor button activates a 3D grid aligned with the 3D tool (hotkey = Shift+P). If you are familiar with other 3D programs, using this option can make you feel more comfortable, providing a better understanding of the 3D tool's position in 3D space. The grid is displayed along the X, Y, or Z axis based on the corresponding button selected. By default, the y-axis grid is activated.

The Local pivot button sets the last edited area of a 3D tool as the center of rotation during editing, which is a helpful function to maintain orientation while manipulating the 3D tool.

The third section of buttons on the right shelf includes the L.Sym and rotation axes controls. These buttons affect how the mesh relates to the virtual sculpting stand and control the rotation of the mesh view on the stand.

The L.Sym button determines how symmetry is calculated while editing a 3D tool. When off, symmetry is calculated in world space based on the center of the virtual sculpting stand. When on, symmetry is calculated based on the center of the mesh, regardless of its position on the stand.

The three buttons below L.Sym control the axis of rotation when changing the mesh view. The XYZ button allows unrestricted rotation in any axis when dragging left or right. The Z button restricts rotation to the z-axis, and the Y button restricts rotation to the y-axis when dragging left or right on the canvas.

The fourth section of buttons on the right shelf controls the display of 3D meshes on the canvas. The Frame button centers the view of the 3D object in the canvas.

Navigating the ZBrush Canvas

Initially, the Move, Scale, and Rotate buttons on the right shelf may be confusing since there are similar buttons on the top shelf, but they serve different purposes. The right shelf buttons are specifically for manipulating 3D tools in Edit mode, allowing you to adjust the view of the 3D tool while working, similar to controls for a virtual sculpture stand. Using these buttons doesn't alter the model itself but affects what you see on the model during work.

To practice navigating the ZBrush canvas with these buttons or the navigation hotkeys, follow these steps:

1. Open Light Box by pressing the comma hotkey or clicking the Light Box button on the top shelf.

2. Navigate to the DemoProjects folder within Projects and load the DemoSoldier project by double-clicking the DemoSoldier.ZPR button.

3. On the left shelf, choose a white color from the color picker to enhance model visibility.

4. On the right shelf, dragging over the Move button will move the soldier model's view. Remember, you're adjusting the view, not the model itself.

5. Holding Alt key and right mouse button (or stylus button on a digital tablet) allows another way to move the view.

6. Dragging over the Scale button on the right shelf will shrink or enlarge the view of the DemoSoldier, just like using a camera's Zoom feature.

7. Holding the right mouse button and Ctrl key while dragging on the canvas achieves the same zoom effect as using the Scale button on the right shelf.

8. Dragging over the Rotate button on the right shelf rotates the view of the soldier.

9. Similarly, dragging on the canvas without holding any keys while right-clicking also rotates the view of the soldier model.

As mentioned earlier, the axis of rotation buttons on the right shelf alters how the Rotate feature behaves. Switching to Z or Y restricts rotation to that specific axis when dragging left or right.

Mesh View Options

The PolyF button enables a wireframe display on the current 3D mesh, showing the individual polygons that form the mesh. If the mesh consists of multiple objects, the wireframe is visible for the active object.

To better understand this feature, you can follow these steps while the DemoSoldier project is loaded:

- Turn on the PolyF button to see the wireframe display with colored regions representing polygroups.

- Rotate the view to reveal the soldier's backpack.

- Alt+click the backpack to view its wireframe.

- The Transp button activates Transparency, allowing you to see the active subtool through other subtools (if the mesh is divided into subtools). There are two transparency modes: Ghost and Standard. By toggling the Ghost button, you can switch between these modes:

- With DemoSoldier on the canvas, turn off PolyF to disable the polyframe display.

- Turn on the Transp button and rotate the view to see the backpack through other parts of the model.

- Turn off Ghost to observe how the Standard transparency mode behaves.

- The Solo button quickly hides all subtools except the current active one, which is useful when working on complex meshes with multiple subtools.

   The Xpose button temporarily moves all subtools aside while keeping them visible. This allows you to focus on editing a single subtool without obstruction and provides insight into how the 3D mesh is organized into subtools.

Trays and Palettes

Located on the right side of the canvas, there is a section called Tool within a large area referred to as the tray. Clicking the divider between the right shelf and the tray collapses the tray, expanding the work area. Clicking it again will make the tray reappear. The tray acts like a drawer in an artist's toolbox and can be found on the right, left, and below the canvas.

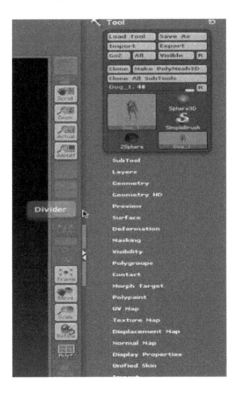

Palettes in ZBrush are sets of controls organized under headings at the top of the interface. For instance, the Document palette contains various settings that control the canvas's appearance and behavior, along with buttons for saving,

35

importing, and exporting images to and from the canvas. To view the settings in the Document palette, simply click the Document button at the top of the interface.

Thee palettes are organized alphabetically at the top of the interface, starting with the Alpha menu on the upper left and ending with the ZScript menu on the upper right. Some palettes are frequently accessed during a ZBrush session, while others are only used occasionally. This is where the trays come in. By clicking the circular icon at the upper-right corner of a palette within the right tray, the palette disappears from the tray and appears beneath the corresponding heading, similar to a menu in conventional software packages. Clicking the circular icon again will return the palette to the right tray. The palette will stay in the tray regardless of whether the tray is open or closed.

To further manage the trays, you can expand or collapse palettes within them. For example, by making sure the Tool palette is in the tray and then expanding the Transform palette, clicking its circular icon in the upper right will move the Transform palette above the Tool palette in the right tray. You can fill the tray with your preferred palettes and remove them by clicking their circular icons, and with practice, this process becomes quick and intuitive. Additionally, clicking the title bar of a palette while it's in the tray will collapse it, creating more room in the tray for other palettes while keeping the collapsed palette available.

The palettes load into the tray from top to bottom in the order they are added. By default, when you click the circular button, palettes will automatically place themselves in the tray on the right side of the screen. If you prefer a palette to be in the tray on the left side, you can grab the handle with your cursor and drag the entire palette to the desired location. When the cursor is over the handle, it turns into a crosshair, indicating that you can drag the palette using the handle.

To rearrange palettes within the tray, you can drag them to different positions. The easiest way to do this is by dragging from the top menu to a blank spot below the last palette in the tray. To remove a palette from the tray, either drag its circular handle icon off the tray or click it. Note that clicking a palette's label in the top menu temporarily hides it from the tray, preventing multiple copies of the same palette from cluttering the tray.

Ensure the Tool palette is in the right tray of the canvas and expanded to view its contents. Clicking the large tool icon in the upper left of the palette will expand the tool inventory. The Tool palette contains numerous subpalettes, which are groups of controls within rounded boxes that appear based on the current tool selection. Some subpalettes are initially collapsed to keep the palette concise. You can expand them by clicking on their labels, such as "Preview" in the Tool palette, which expands the Preview settings in their own subpalette.

If several subpalettes are expanded, the Tool palette may become too long to fit on the screen. In that case, you can click the side of the Tool palette and drag up and down to scroll and access all the different settings.

Throughout this book, specific controls' locations will be described in relation to the subpalettes of a particular palette. For instance, if directed to find the "SDiv" slider in the Geometry subpalette of the Tool palette, you should expand the Tool palette and then the Geometry subpalette to locate the "SDiv" slider. This distinction is essential as there are some subpalettes with the same names as a palette, like the Texture palette and the Texture Map subpalette within the Tool palette.

Now that you have a grasp of how palettes and trays function, let's explore the settings available in each palette briefly.

- **Alpha:** This palette contains controls for fine-tuning the appearance and behavior of alphas, grayscale image files used for various purposes in ZBrush. The alpha icon on the left shelf opens the alpha fly-out library. You can also access the library of alphas by clicking the image of the alpha in the upper left of the Alpha palette.

- **Brush:** The Brush palette contains numerous controls that modify the behavior of sculpting brushes. These controls are arranged in sub palettes and can be used to create your own custom brush presets, which can be utilized in future ZBrush sessions. You can access the brush fly-out library by clicking the brush icon in the upper left of the palette.

- **Color:** This palette replicates the color picker found on the left shelf and includes additional pickers and controls within the Modifiers subpalette.

- **Document:** In the Document palette, you can load and save ZBrush documents, import and export Photoshop files, and other supported formats like BMP, JPEG, and TIFF. This palette also offers controls for setting background gradient colors, border colors, and document size. Use the Pro button to maintain the current aspect ratio when resizing the document. Adjust the document size at the beginning of your work since resizing while creating a composition will clear the canvas.

- **Draw:** The Draw palette duplicates brush controls from the top shelf, including size, focal shift, material and color settings, and brush depth controls (Zadd, Zsub, and Zcut). It also provides a subpalette for previewing brush strokes in 2.5D Paint mode, not for altering 3D models in Edit mode. The preview shows how the brush tip appears on the ZBrush canvas, allowing you to adjust width, height, and depth of the brush tip and how the stroke embeds into existing strokes on the canvas. These settings affect all brushes used in a ZBrush session, serving as global controls for stroke appearance.

Additionally, the Draw palette includes buttons like Persp and Floor, which work similarly to the ones on the right shelf, with added controls. The Focal Length slider influences perspective distortion when the Persp button is on. The Align To Object button maintains the perspective distortion of the 3D tool relative to its location on the canvas. There are also controls for setting grid display position and colors activated when the Floor button is on.

- **Edit:** This palette provides access to Undo and Redo buttons, displaying the number of available undos. The undo hotkeys are Ctrl+Z for undo and Ctrl+Shift+Z for redo. You can adjust the number of undos stored in memory using the sliders in the Mem subpalette of the Preferences palette. Increasing the Tool Undo slider (default set to 4) allows more undos during sculpting. Further details about the Preferences palette will be covered later in this section.

- **File:** The File palette contains buttons for saving different elements of your ZBrush session. You can use the Save As button at the top of the palette to save a ZBrush project in the ZPR format. This format preserves the current active 3D mesh, its position on the canvas, the tool's state (Edit mode or not), materials, and canvas background color. The Load button allows you to load saved ZBrush projects, and Revert sets the project back to its last saved state.

In addition, the File palette includes buttons that duplicate the Save functionality found in other palettes. For example, the Save button under Canvas duplicates the Save button in the Document palette, saving strokes drawn on the canvas without the current 3D mesh. Similarly, the Save button under Tool Mesh saves the current 3D tool (while in Edit mode) without any canvas strokes.

Initially, it might be confusing to remember what to save or load in ZBrush. A safe approach is to use the Save button at the top of the File palette to save the entire ZBrush project. This way, when you reopen ZBrush using the Open button in the File palette, you can resume right where you left off. Saving the project in the ZProjects folder within the Pixologic folder will list your saved files under the Projects setting in Light Box.

- **Layer:** ZBrush supports layers in a document, similar to layers in paint programs like Photoshop. However, unlike traditional 2D paint program layers where one layer obscures all layers beneath it, ZBrush layers respect the depth of all strokes equally. Layers are commonly used in ZBrush as an illustration program.

- **Light:** The Light palette allows you to adjust the settings for the current light, create additional lights, and modify shadows and shadow types. You can reposition a light by dragging the cursor over the material preview sphere, which updates to show the lighting position in the scene. This flexibility to change lighting while working in ZBrush is a valuable feature, as it allows artists to reveal potential issues or explore new artistic possibilities.

ZBrush's lighting capabilities have significantly improved in recent versions, enabling the creation of photorealistic lighting setups within the software.

- **Macro:** The Macro palette provides controls for recording and loading macros. A macro is essentially a list of commands that instruct ZBrush to perform specific actions. For instance, if you frequently reset the document size to a particular resolution, you can record a macro to execute this action, and it will appear as a button in the Macro palette. Clicking the button will replay the recorded actions, resizing the document according to your specified settings.

- **Marker:** Markers in ZBrush are used to store information about a 3D tool's position on the canvas before it is dropped. This allows you to redraw the tool later on, even after making changes to the composition. The Marker palette's buttons determine what information is stored on the canvas, and markers serve as hot spots for this purpose. While the Multi-marker tool allows creating groups of 3D tools stored as a single tool, the introduction of subtools in ZBrush 3 has made this feature less significant.

- **Material:** In ZBrush, material refers to the surface quality and how it reacts to light, shadow, and other elements in the scene. There are two main types of materials: MatCap, which come with built-in lighting and shading, and standard materials. Know that the Material palette is where you can edit, load, save, and clone materials used in a scene. The Modifiers subpalette provides controls to customize existing material presets and save them for future projects.

- **Movie:** The Movie palette includes controls for recording movies from the canvas. You can make movies to showcase your work or demonstrate specific techniques, or use them for presenting ideas to clients or directors. The recorded movies can be exported in

QuickTime format for easy sharing, and the Movie palette allows you to create turntable animations, which are useful for displaying your work from various angles.

- **Picker:** The Picker palette controls how brushes sample information when interacting with strokes and 3D meshes on the canvas, significantly affecting sculpting brush behavior.

- **Preferences:** The Preferences palette is where you customize the overall behavior of ZBrush. It contains settings for interface customization, 3D model import behavior, and more. We'll revisit this palette throughout the book to explore how these controls can enhance your interaction with ZBrush.

- **Render:** The Render palette provides controls for lighting, shading, anti-aliasing, and other rendering aspects of your ZBrush composition. Rendering in ZBrush occurs directly on the canvas, unlike other 3D programs. The Render palette offers various quality settings, including Preview, Fast, Flat, and Best. Best quality rendering is computationally intensive, considering lighting, texturing, shadows, and material interactions, such as reflection and light occlusion.

- **Texture:** The Texture palette, similar to the Alpha palette, allows you to load, save, and adjust textures. Textures are 2D color images used for various purposes in ZBrush, such as painting 3D tools or exporting as texture maps for 3D animation and rendering programs.

- **Tool:** The Tool palette is the core of ZBrush, essential for digital sculpting and painting. It houses various paintbrushes, 3D meshes, and special tools like ZSpheres. The inventory is divided into three sections: Quick Pick for easy access to recently used tools, 3D Meshes containing loaded models and primitives, and 2.5D Brushes mainly used for illustration and canvas adjustments. With hundreds of controls and sliders, this palette allows importing/exporting 3D meshes, adding parts, painting colors, animating, creating UV texture coordinates, and much more. The Tool palette becomes your primary workspace in ZBrush, especially when working on meshes in Edit mode.

- **Transform:** The Transform palette duplicates buttons found on the shelves, such as Draw, Edit, Move, Scale, and Rotate. However, its key feature is symmetry settings. Used during 3D mesh editing, symmetry accelerates the sculpting process by allowing simultaneous work on both sides of the mesh.

- **Zplugin:** The Zplugin palette provides access to ZBrush plug-ins, links to ZBrush-related sites, license editing, and help files. ZPlugins offer various additional features to explore.

- **ZScript:** ZBrush includes a built-in scripting language called ZScript. ZScripts can be simple macros or functional plug-ins with custom interfaces. They can be recorded through the interface using the palette's controls or by typing commands into a text file.

The title bar

The title bar is located at the upper-left side of the screen. It displays valuable information such as the document title, registration details, memory usage, and session duration.

On the right side of the title bar, you'll find helpful buttons. The first one, labeled Menus, toggles the visibility of menus. The second button, DefaultZScript, allows you to load custom zscripts.

CHAPTER 3: SURFACE NOISE, LAYERS, AND THE ZBRUSH TIMELINE

Surface Noise

ZBrush employs a special effect on the exposed sections of a mesh, which is then projected onto sculpted geometry. It results in intricate detailing even on a lower-resolution mesh. Additionally, you can permanently integrate the noise into the mesh, blending it with your surface sculpted details.

Surface noise serves various purposes, and its application to the mesh is straightforward. The noise is procedurally generated, meaning it arises from intricate algorithms. ZBrush handles complex calculations and offers a user-friendly interface for adjusting the overall visual outcome. The NoiseMaker plug-in expands the options for crafting your noise and can be accessed via the Surface Noise interface.

The provided exercises cover the fundamental steps of generating surface noise while showcasing innovative applications of this tool.

Making Some Noise

Let's quickly explore the Surface Noise interface using a basic PolySphere as our example mesh:

1. Launch ZBrush and open the DefaultSphere.ZPR project from the Projects section in LightBox.

2. Set the color to white and apply the BasicMaterial2 material for better visibility of noise effects on the sphere.

3. In the Tool palette, access the Surface subpalette.

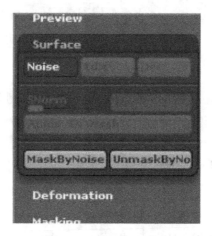

4. Click the Noise button, triggering the appearance of the Surface Noise interface, where you'll configure the noise's appearance.

   On the interface's left side, a preview window showcases noise adjustments on the mesh in real time as you modify settings. Drag within the window to rotate the view. For zooming, drag left/right on "Zoom" at the upper right, and for view movement, drag on "Move" at the lower right. Click "Frame" at the upper left to focus the view.

The "Save" button stores settings in .znm format, while "Open" loads saved settings for future use. It helps in building a library of noise configurations across projects.

The "Copy" button memorizes settings, which is useful when transferring noise setups between subtools or tools. The right side houses sliders, controls, and the familiar ZBrush edit curve, where most adjustments occur. Achieving desired noise effects involves experimenting with these sliders.

The "Scale" slider modifies the overall noise scale, and "Strength" adjusts noise amplitude. Negative "Strength" values invert noise direction (pushing outward instead of inward).

"Magnify By Mask" changes noise scale for masked areas, while "Strength By Mask" adjusts noise strength in masked versus unmasked regions.

"ColorBlend" introduces a tint to noise. Two color pickers below the slider set the tint color: right for slider right-push, left for slider left-push.

The edit curve customizes noise intensity nonlinearly across the surface. It's a creative playground—I often spend hours tinkering with the edit curve when working with surface noise. To understand it better, experiment with the graph. Try the following to simulate a rocky asteroid appearance.

5. Adjust the Scale slider to approximately 100 and set the Strength slider to roughly 0.01.

6. Place a point on the left side of the graph by clicking on the curve, then move this point up and down to observe the resulting change on the surface. A multitude of design variations can be achieved by experimenting with the graph.

    The offset, angle, and scale sliders beneath the preview window offer further possibilities to fine-tune the noise appearance, controlling these aspects along the specified axis.

7. When content with the outcome, click the OK button at the interface's bottom. This action causes the noise to be projected onto the mesh.

    It's crucial to realize that, at this stage, the noise is projected onto the mesh without altering its polygons. Think of it like a bump map, creating the illusion of greater sculpted detail on the mesh than exists. It becomes evident when the SDiv slider is set to a low value, revealing the projected detail atop the surface polygons.

8. You should modify the noise appearance even after exiting the Surface Noise editor. To do so, click the Edit button within the Surface subpalette of the Tool palette.

Using the Noise button in the Surface Palette, you can toggle noise visibility on or off, while the Del button eliminates the noise settings.

Applying the Noise to Your Mesh

This technique can be handy for quickly adding detail. You can even pre-apply masking to determine where the noise should be used. This example demonstrates adding a rocky texture to a gargoyle model's unmasked areas.

1. Open ZBrush and load the project on the DVD. This project contains a simple gargoyle model with a Notre Dame–style sculpt created using Dynamesh.

2. Adjust the SDiv slider in the Tool palette to 2, giving the model around 2.5 million points. It ensures enough points to support the noise detail incorporated into the mesh. While you can apply noise to the entire mesh, it's more realistic to mask parts of the surface for uneven noise distribution. Masking should be done before applying the noise. A suggested approach is to use a mask based on surface smoothness. It will protect hard edges from the noise, making them appear smoother than the rest of the surface, contributing to a weathered look.

3. Go to the Masking subpalette in the Tool palette. Adjust the Range slider next to the Mask By Smooth button 250 and set Falloff to 300.

These high settings increase the mask's spread and smoothness. Click the Mask By Smooth button to see the mask appear on the surface edges.

4. Expand the Surface subpalette and click the Noise button to access the Surface Noise subpalette. Set Strength to 0.001. Increase the Scale to approximately 30 for a stony texture. Set ColorBlend to 0 to show only the noise deformation, not the color effect.

5. Play around with the graph adjustments. Zoom in slightly on the preview window while tweaking the settings to observe the changes.

6. Avoid making the noise overly intense; otherwise, the surface will bulge oddly when you implement it on the

mesh. Also, ensure that the scale is a manageable size. If the noise is excellent, the surface will appear fuzzy. The desired outcome is something resembling stone.

7. Once you have a result you're satisfied with, click the OK button. The noise will become visible on the canvas's surface. However, it's only projected at this stage and hasn't been integrated into the mesh.

8. Before applying the noise to the mesh, adjust the SNormal slider in the Surface subpalette to 100. It guarantees smooth surface normals when the noise is used, enhancing its appearance. You can experiment with lower values for a crisper noise effect.

9. Click the Apply To Mesh button. After a brief period, you'll notice that the noise has been incorporated into the mesh. With a sufficiently high-resolution surface and reasonable noise strength, you should achieve a visually pleasing noise effect resembling stone.

10. To remove the mask, Ctrl+drag on the canvas. Observe that the areas that were masked remain smooth.

11. Achieving the ideal settings might require some effort, but there's a technique that simplifies applying surface noise.

12. Save the project as "gargoyleNoise.ZPR." We'll revisit this model in the upcoming sections as we further experiment with noise.

Using an Image to Make Noise

It's possible to employ an image to dictate the appearance of the noise on the surface, expanding the creative potential of noise. To achieve a highly stony appearance for the gargoyle, let's explore the outcome of using a rocky texture to influence the noise design.

We'll observe how this textured noise interacts when layered over the noise generated in the previous section:

1. Once again, initiate by applying a mask. While this step isn't obligatory when working with noise, it adds an intriguing dimension to the appearance.

2. Continue working with the same gargoyle model as in the preceding section.

3. Adjust the Range slider next to the Mask By Smooth button in the Masking subpalette to 30, and set Falloff to 100. Create the mask by clicking Mask By Smooth.

4. Next, select a suitable rocky texture for the noise image. You can source one from the Internet or choose from the textures available in LightBox. Open LightBox and navigate to the Textures section to browse the images. An example I prefer is IMG_4959.jpg. Note down the file path to this image on your hard drive; it's displayed at the bottom of LightBox.

5. Expand the Surface subpalette within the Tool palette and click the Noise button. This action reverts to the previous noise settings saved in memory. However, we intend to establish new settings. Click Edit to access the Surface Noise interface.

6. To employ an image for generating noise, toggle the Alpha On/Off button at the lower left.

7. When you click on the image, a browser window appears. Use this to locate the image based on the file path displayed in LightBox. For instance, the desired

image, such as IMG_4959.jpg, can be found in the ZBrush R3/ZTextures folder. Of course, you can choose any image, but this one yields a pleasing effect.

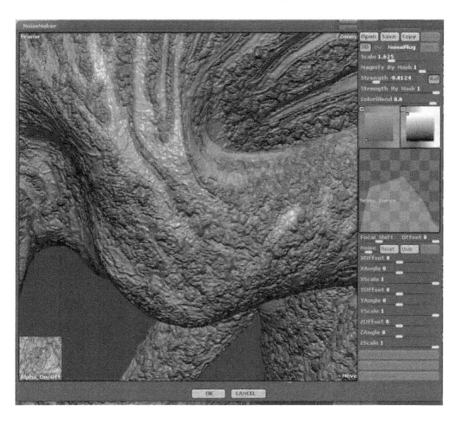

8. The image has been loaded, although the impact might not be easily discernible. To enhance the effect, make slight adjustments to the settings. I achieved optimal outcomes by reducing the scale to 1.625 and the strength to -0.0124. Afterward, I refined the Strength parameter through experimentation using the curve editor. Remember that you can create a distinct angle in the

graph by dragging one of the points on the curve of the editor and then returning it.

9. When you arrive at a favorable outcome, click the OK button to close the interface. Subsequently, elevate the SNormal slider in the Surface subpalette to 100 and select Apply To Mesh.

10. Clear the mask by performing a Ctrl+drag action on the canvas and evaluate the outcomes. The gargoyle's appearance is undeniably more stone-like.

Morph Targets

Targets are a recognizable element within various 3D animation software. For instance, in Autodesk® Maya®, they are called blend shapes. Animators frequently employ morph targets to retain the vertex positions of a 3D model. These positions are then interpolated to craft and animate facial expressions.

ZBrush enables the creation of a singular morph target for your 3D tool. When your tool comprises multiple subtools, you also have the choice to create a morph target for each subtool if desired.

Morph targets in ZBrush are uncomplicated to generate and utilize. This simplicity renders them perfect for testing facial expressions and basic animation. Furthermore, they save the model's initial state, offering a way to restore the model even when undo options are exhausted.

Storing a Morph Target

A morph target stores the vertex positions of a model in memory, effectively becoming a part of the model. ZBrush retains this state in memory until the morph target is deleted. Even after saving and closing the file, reopening it later preserves the morph target information, serving as a safety net to revert to the original model state during development.

You can manage morph targets through the Morph Target subpalette within the Tool palette. Each active subtool can have one morph target at a time. For more complex variations, using 3D layers is recommended.

Here's how to save a morph target:

1.   Launch ZBrush.

2. Open the brainGuy.ZPR project using the Open button in the File menu. Ensure the head of the humanoid character is on the canvas and in Edit mode.

3. Access the Morph Target subpalette in the Tool palette.

4. Ensure the Head subtool is active (lighter color on the canvas). You can select it by Alt+clicking on the head.

5. Click the StoreMT button to save the current model state as a morph target. The other buttons in the subpalette will become available, and the StoreMT button will be grayed out, indicating the presence of a saved morph target.

6. While a morph target is saved, you can continue working on other subdivision levels. Switching to a different subdivision level will turn off all buttons except the DelMT button until you return to the level where the morph target was stored.

7. You can proceed with the next section using the same file.

Switching Targets

Once a morph target is saved, any modifications made after storing it won't be included in the saved information. You can toggle between your changes and the stored morph target using the Switch button in the Morph Target subpalette within the Tool palette.

Here's how this process functions: A morph target was saved for the Head subtool at the current subdivision level in the prior section. The grayed-out StoreMT button in the Morph Target subpalette confirms the presence of a stored subtool.

- Access the sculpting brush library and pick the Move brush.

- Increase the Draw Size to 70 and significantly alter the face, such as pulling the eyebrows down using the brush.

- Click the Switch button in the Morph Target subpalette of the Tool palette. This action reverts the head to its initial state.

- Click the Switch button again, causing the brows to return to their lowered position.

- Adjust the Morph slider to the right to raise the brows, and slide it left to lower them even further than their original state.

- While using morph targets, it's important to be mindful of the state you're working on. Morph targets store two states: the initial stored state (created when the StoreMT button was pressed) and the modified state (resulting from changes made after pressing the StoreMT button). Any alterations performed in the stored state will become part of the saved morph target.

- The CreateDiff button generates a fresh mesh reflecting the disparity between the stored and modified states. This mesh is stored in the Tool inventory and labeled with the prefix "MorphDiff" attached.

- The Project Morph button relaxes the mesh based on the stored morph target, addressing issues like pinching and stretching while retaining surface details.

- You can proceed with the subsequent section using the same file.

Deleting a Morph Target

You can access this option anytime to make your modifications permanent or to free up space for another morph target.

To remove a morph target, press the DelMT button within the Morph Target subpalette located in the Tool palette. This action solidifies the current model state, meaning any changes applied to the model after storing a morph target are locked in. Any changes you make will be erased if you return to the stored state and then delete the morph target.

Here's how to proceed:

1. Click the Switch button to restore the model to its original state before any adjustments are made to the brows.

2. Click the DelMT button.

The other buttons in the Morph Target subpalette of the Tool palette will be grayed out, indicating that the model no longer retains a stored morph target.

3. You can proceed with the next section using the same file.

Using the Morph Brush

It is a specialized sculpting tool designed to return particular parts of a model to their saved morph target state. This brush offers creative possibilities and can be an ultimate "Undo" tool. If you're not satisfied with changes made to a specific part of the model, you can carefully use the Morph brush to undo those modifications.

Here's how to use the Morph brush:

1. Make sure the head is currently chosen as the subtotal.

2. Click on the StoreMT button in the Morph Target subpalette located within the Tool palette.

3. Utilize the Move tool to push the eyebrows upwards. It's acceptable to be imprecise, as this might also lift the upper eyelids.

4. Access the sculpting brush collection and select the Morph brush.

5. Reduce the Draw Size to 20 and set Z Intensity to 10. Decreasing these values improves accuracy when applying the morph to specific areas.

6. Zoom in on the model. Brush over the stretched section of the eyelids.

7. This action will cause the upper eyelids to return to their original position. Using the brush, you can address problematic areas while sculpting facial expressions. It's always recommended to save a morph target when editing your model to conveniently fix issues like stretched regions.

Using 3D Layers

The Layers Subpalette

You'll discover all the controls necessary for managing layers in the Tool palette's Layers subpalette.

A layer is only possible when the model is at its highest subdivision level; otherwise, a warning will appear. In this exercise, you'll learn how to generate a 3D layer:

1. Initiate a fresh ZBrush session.

2. Employ the Open button in the File palette to load the BrainGuy.ZPR project on the DVD.

3. Confirm that the head is presently the selected subtool.

Within the Layers subpalette, initiate a new layer by clicking the large box button.

4. The top slot in the Layers subpalette is now highlighted. It's marked as Untitled Layer 1, and you'll observe the enabled record button labeled REC.

5. Click the Name button in the Layers subpalette and enter "Pores." It establishes a personalized name for the layer, now identified as Pores1.

6. Assigning names to layers is recommended, as the Layers subpalette can swiftly become populated with numerous layers. With proper names, identifying the stored information within each layer becomes easier.

7. Utilize the Save button in the File palette to save the project.

8. Proceed with this saved file in the following section.

Layer Record Mode

When a new layer is generated, it automatically enters Record mode. It is indicated by the REC label on the right side of the layer slot within the Layers subpalette of the Tool palette. Any modifications conducted on the model during Record mode are stored within that specific layer. Recording can only be performed on a single layer at a time. If a new layer is created while an existing layer is in Record mode, the initial layer stops recording, and the newly added layer enters Record mode. Subsequent changes made to the model are then recorded within the new layer.

To deactivate Record mode, click the REC button on the right side of the layer slot. The REC label will deactivate, and the eyeball icon will appear. The eyeball icon regulates the layer's visibility.

While it is feasible to deactivate Record mode for all layers and proceed with model adjustments, maintaining consistent use of layers is advisable. It ensures effective tracking of the changes stored within each layer.

Layer Strength

It is possible to record alterations in a layer and subsequently adjust its intensity as needed. This feature holds considerable value for a broad range of applications. For instance, I frequently employ this technique to modify the intensity of surface noise after it has been applied to a surface. As observed in the preceding discussion on surface noise, there are instances where the outcome upon applying noise to the surface isn't as anticipated – the model might expand, or the noise could be excessively intense or subtle. Utilizing layers alongside surface noise can achieve a higher degree of control over the outcome.

1. Utilize the project you saved in the prior section.

2. There's currently a single layer called "Pores" in Record mode, denoted by "REC" in the Layers subpalette of the Tool palette. This layer adds noise to the model's surface, creating a pattern throughout the selected subtool.

3. Go to the Surface subpalette of the Tool palette and activate the Noise button.

4. Adjust the Noise Scale to 0.5 and Strength to 0.025.

5. Press the Apply To Mesh button in the Surface subpalette of the Tool palette. The noise pattern is now incorporated into the mesh. Since the REC button is enabled in the Pores1 layer, the applied noise is contained in this layer.

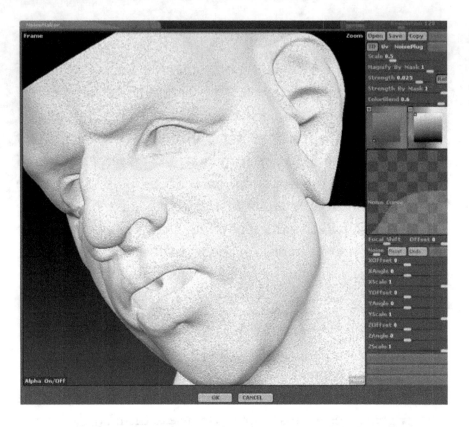

6. Click the eye icon to hide the pores' visibility, making the noise vanish.

7. Click the eye icon again to restore the Noise layer, bringing back the noise. When the layer is invisible, deformations on the layer are concealed but not erased.

8. Adjust the Pores slider in the Layers subpalette to alter the layer's strength. Set the Pores slider below the layer stack to 0.2. The noise pattern is less prominent, with a decreased slider value. Also, note that the slider next to

the Pores1 layer in the layer stack can also adjust the layer's strength.

9. Set the Pores slider to 1.2. The noise becomes more intense.

10. You can increase the slider strength beyond 1 to enhance the changes saved in the layer. You can even invert the layer's appearance with a negative slider value.

11. Use the Save option in the File menu to save the project.

Baking Layers

Changes made using layers can be made permanent by baking the layers. In this case, you'll improve the appearance of the pores and then introduce wrinkles on a new layer. These alterations will become a lasting part of the model.

1. Proceed with the file from the preceding section.

   The pores require slight smoothing for a more realistic look. The SmoothPeaks brush is effective for this purpose. You'll find this brush in the Brush/Smooth section of LightBox.

2. Open LightBox and navigate to the Brush section. Find and open the Smooth folder. Locate the SmoothPeaks brush.

3. Double-click the SmoothPeaks brush. Note the warning about mapping the brush to the Shift key.

4. Choose the Pores1 layer and set the Pores slider to 0.5.

5. In the Layers subpalette of the Tool palette, create a new layer using the large square button with a plus sign in the Layers subpalette. Name this layer "SmoothPores."

6. To ensure you can smooth without issues, create the "SmoothPores" layer. It is crucial when there are active deformation layers. You can either revert the original Pores layer to Record mode or record the smoothing in a new layer. The latter provides flexibility for adjusting strength, hence it's recommended. Creating "SmoothPores" switches the Pores1 layer out of Record mode.

7. Enlarge the view. Set the Draw Size to 60 for faster work.

8. Press Shift and adjust the Z Intensity slider to 40. Use the brush to smooth the face's noise. This setting evens

out the noise without erasing it. Hold Shift and brush over the surface to make the pores look more realistic, thanks to the SmoothPeaks brush.

The Smooth Peaks brush smooths raised areas, creating a skin-pore-like effect on a noisy surface.

9. Brush over the head's entire surface. Vary the brush strength for smoother results in some areas, adding variety.

10. The pores might still appear exaggerated, but that's fine. You can adjust the Pores layer's strength and experiment with the Pores and SmoothPores layers.

After smoothing the head, create a new layer named "Wrinkles" in the Layers subpalette of the Tool palette.

For wrinkles, use the Dam_Standard brush. It's suitable for creating fine lines, scratches, and wrinkles.

11. Select the Dam_Standard brush from the Brush palette.

12. Employ the brush to craft wrinkles and fine lines around the eyes and skin folds.

13. Once enough wrinkles are added, turn off Record mode by clicking the REC button in the Wrinkles layer slot in the Layers subpalette of the Tool palette.

14. Experiment with Pores, SmoothPores, and Wrinkles layers' slider values.

15. Permanently save your work before baking layers. Use the Save button in the File palette and save the file.

16. In the Layers subpalette, click the Bake All button.

    The Bake All button solidifies changes in each layer, making them permanent. The slider values determine layer strength during baking.

    To remove a layer and its changes, click the Delete Layer button in the Layers subpalette of the Tool palette.

    Baking layers depend on your goals in ZBrush. Layers aid in testing ideas during sculpting and offer variations for presenting to directors or clients.

CONCLUSION

Zbrush for Beginner's serves as a thorough and valuable aid for individuals aiming to grasp the foundations of this robust 3D sculpting software. Within its pages, the authors adeptly explain the diverse array of tools and features ZBrush offers, providing practical instances and step-by-step tutorials to facilitate your mastery of the program.

Whether you're just starting or have intermediate experience, the Beginner's Guide to ZBrush is an excellent stepping stone for those interested in comprehending the basics of 3D sculpting. The book delves into everything from understanding the user interface and basic sculpting techniques to venturing into more advanced subjects such as texturing, rendering, and animation.

This guide benefits artists and designers aspiring to enhance their abilities and craft breathtaking 3D models and artwork. With its user-friendly interface and potent capabilities, ZBrush has evolved into an indispensable instrument for anyone venturing into 3D artwork, and this book will aid in unlocking its full potential.

We sincerely hope this guide has proven to be a valuable asset, helping you gain a solid grasp of ZBrush's fundamentals. Always remember the possibilities with ZBrush are boundless, so continue to explore and uncover novel methods of producing stunning 3D creations.

.

www.ingramcontent.com/pod-product-compliance
Lightning Source LLC
LaVergne TN
LVHW051606050326
832903LV00033B/4388